KV-676-083

Winnie's Outdoor Fun

LAURA OWEN & KORKY PAUL

OXFORD
UNIVERSITY PRESS

Helping your child to read

Before they start

* Talk about the back cover blurb. What kinds of things might you find in a magical garden?
* Look at the cover picture. Does it give any clues about what might happen in the stories?

During reading

* Let your child read at their own pace, either silently or out loud.
* If necessary, help them work out words they don't know by saying each sound out loud and then blending them to say the word, e.g. *a-b-s-o-l-ute-l-y, absolutely*.
* Encourage your child to keep checking that the text makes sense and they understand what they are reading. Remind them to reread to check the meaning if they're not sure.
* Give them lots of praise for good reading!

After reading

* Look at page 48 for some fun activities.

Contents

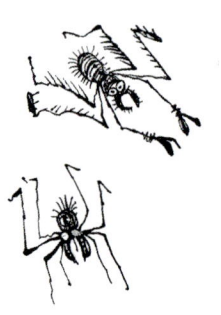

OXFORD
UNIVERSITY PRESS

Great Clarendon Street, Oxford OX2 6DP
Oxford University Press is a department of the University of Oxford.
It furthers the University's objective of excellence in research, scholarship,
and education by publishing worldwide. Oxford is a registered trade mark
of Oxford University Press in the UK and in certain other countries

Text © Oxford University Press
Illustrations © Korky Paul
The characters in this work are the original creation of Valerie Thomas
who retains copyright in the characters.

"Blooming Winnie" was first published in *Giddy-Up Winnie* 2010
"Winnie the Twit" was first published in *Winnie the Twit* 2010
This edition published 2018

The moral rights of the author/illustrator have been asserted

Database right Oxford University Press (maker)

All rights reserved. No part of this publication may be reproduced,
stored in a retrieval system, or transmitted, in any form or by any means,
without the prior permission in writing of Oxford University Press,
or as expressly permitted by law, or under terms agreed with the appropriate
reprographics rights organization. Enquiries concerning reproduction
outside the scope of the above should be sent to the Rights Department,
Oxford University Press, at the address above

You must not circulate this book in any other binding or cover
and you must impose this same condition on any acquirer

British Library Cataloguing in Publication Data

Data available

ISBN: 978-0-19-276524-6

3 5 7 9 10 8 6 4 2

Printed in China

Paper used in the production of this book is a natural,
recyclable product made from wood grown in sustainable forests.
The manufacturing process conforms to the environmental
regulations of the country of origin.

Acknowledgements
With thanks to Catherine Baker for editorial support

Blooming Winnie

6

⭐ Chapter ⭐ One

Squeaky-squeaky-squeak-eek!

"Is that a mouse?" said Winnie, with her mouth full of toast and mildew marmalade. "Oh no, it's just my moaning phone! Wilbur must have changed the ringtone again!" Winnie snatched the phone from her pocket and put it to her ear. "Hello?" she said.

A ladylike voice on the phone said, "This is Mrs Parmar from the school. Can I ask you a favour, Winnie?"

"That depends what it is," said Winnie.

"Could the children come and look at the plants and creatures in your garden?" said Mrs Parmar. "They're doing a project."

"Oooh, that would be lovely!"
said Winnie.

"There is one rule!" said Mrs Parmar
sternly. "You must absolutely do absolutely
no magic while the children are absolutely
with you."

"Easy-peasy, pink-worm-squeezy!"
said Winnie.

"I'm trusting you, Winnie!" said
Mrs Parmar. "I'll bring the children at
two o'clock."

9

"Yippee!" said Winnie. But then she looked out of the window. "Oh dear," she said. "I'd forgotten what a tangle-mangle the garden is."

Winnie pulled her wand from her sleeve. "We've just got time to do some magic gardening before the children arrive," she said. "Come on, Wilbur!"

⭐ Chapter ✖ Two

Wilbur followed her outside.

"The children will want to see frilly flowery, sweet-smelly, brightly coloured plants in the garden," said Winnie, waving her wand. "**Abracadabra!**"

Instantly, Winnie was wearing the most frilly flowery, sweet-smelly, brightly coloured shoes you've ever seen.

"Oh, bats' toenails!" said Winnie crossly. "What's gone wrong?"

Wilbur pointed at Winnie's wand. It was bent.

"This wand is pointing to the wrong thing!" said Winnie. "Let's try again! **Abracadabra!**"

Instantly, the big black crows in the garden became frilly flowery, sweet-smelly, brightly coloured birds.

Winnie tried to straighten the wand, but it just wilted. "What in the witchy world is wrong with my wand?" said Winnie. She shook the wand, but it stayed all bent and wilted. She put a bandage on the wand. She dipped the wand in medicine. But it still stayed wilted.

"I've run out of ideas," said Winnie.

"I know, I'll have a look in Great Aunt Winifred's *Book of All Things Magic*. Maybe she knows how to cure it."

Winnie opened the dusty book and looked at the spells inside.

"Oh, botheration!" she said. "There are so many to choose from! Where should I start? Oh, I wish my Great Aunt Winifred could help me!"

"Cheer up, girl!" said a dusty old voice.

14

Cough, cough!

"Oooh!" said Winnie.

"Hiss!" went Wilbur. All his fur stood up on end.

Suddenly, Winnie's Great Aunt Winifred appeared like grey fog floating over the table.

"What's your problem, girl?" she boomed. Winnie suddenly felt nervous. "Ug, er, gulp," said Winnie. It sounded as if she had forgotten how to talk.

"Come on! Spit it out!" said Great Aunt Winifred.

Winnie suddenly found her voice again. "It's my wand," she said. "It's wilted."

"Easy! Just give it some Booster's Wand Food!" said Great Aunt Winifred.

"I tried that," said Winnie, gloomily. "I've tried everything. But nothing seems to work!"

"Don't despair, girl," said Great Aunt
Winifred. "Just grow yourself a new wand."

"But how?" said Winnie.

"It's as easy as picking fleas from a fairy
cake," said Winifred. "Stick your wand into
some soil. Water it. Watch it grow. It's as
simple as that."

"Wow," said Winnie. "I never knew."

⭐ Chapter ⭐
Three

Winnie planted her wilted wand, and
watered it. At once it began to grow. As
it got bigger, new wands grew on it – fat
wands, thin wands, knobbly wands, curvy
wands, wibbly wobbly wands.

"Just pick one good straight wand,"
said Great Aunt Winifred, floating
behind Winnie.

Winnie was just reaching out to pick a
perfect wand when suddenly, they heard
something.

"Sounds like a hundred screeching baby
owls just popped from their eggs," said Great
Aunt Winifred, covering her ears.

"It's the children!" said Winnie. "Get into
the house, Auntie! They mustn't see you!"

The children trooped into the garden with
Mrs Parmar. "I'll be back at three o'clock,
Winnie," said Mrs Parmar. "Have a good
afternoon, and remember …"

"Absolutely no magic!" said Winnie.
"I know."

But the children didn't know about
that rule. They weren't interested in the
giant apple-crumble tree crawling with
cattypillars. They weren't interested in
stinking nettles or biggle-bugs.

No. The children ran straight to the wand tree and began picking wands, and waving them around.

"Oh, please stop!" said Winnie, but nobody was listening. "Oh, slithering slugs, what shall I do, Wilbur?"

But Wilbur wasn't there. Instead, Winnie saw a tiny, sad-looking black mammoth.

"Wilbur!" cried Winnie. "Oh, please, children, don't ..."

Zip! Zap! Ting! Splosh! Zob!

Magic was flying everywhere! Plants were being changed. Children were being changed. Winnie was being changed!

Then Great Aunt Winifred came roaring to the rescue. "Stop that! At once!" she bellowed.

The children froze.

"Place all your wands on the ground!" boomed Great Aunt Winifred. "Now, line up, two by two. No talking!"

Great Aunt Winifred picked up a straight wand. "**Abracadabra!**"

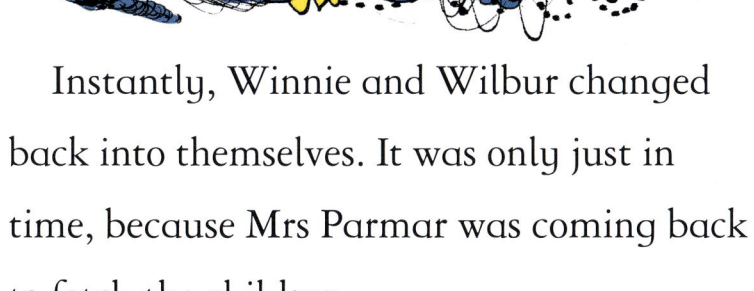

Instantly, Winnie and Wilbur changed back into themselves. It was only just in time, because Mrs Parmar was coming back to fetch the children.

"Oh, my goodness!" said Mrs Parmar. "The children are being well-behaved!"

"I've not done any magic all afternoon," said Winnie.

"Good!" said Mrs Parmar. "Back to school, then, children!"

"Shall we have a bonfire of all those wands?" said Winnie as the children left.

So Winnie and Wilbur and Great Aunt
Winifred made a bonfire. It burned and
sparkled with all the colours of the rainbow
and magic sounds crackled from it. They
all toasted squishy marshmallows over
the flames.

At bedtime, Great Aunt Winifred began to nag Winnie. "Brush your hair properly! And make sure you brush your teeth for at least five minutes! Have you polished your nose?"

"Time to go back into your book, Auntie," said Winnie. "Nighty-night!" Winnie slammed the book shut, and then there was silence. "That's better!" she said.

"Meeow!" agreed Wilbur.

Winnie
the Twit

★ Chapter ★
One

Wilbur and Winnie were in the garden,
picking fresh cattypillars off the pongberry
trees to eat.

"How many cattypillars have you got,
Wilbur?" asked Winnie, munching.

Wilbur showed her his bucket of
wriggling, hairy cattypillars.

"Oooh, well done, Wilbur! Yummy!"
said Winnie.

She opened her mouth wide, like a baby bird, and threw a cattypillar in.

"Mmm. I should stop eating cattypillars or there won't be enough to make the jam. But they are so delicious!" Winnie picked out the bits of cattypillar stuck to her teeth. "Isn't nature wonderful, Wilbur?" she said. "It gives us everything we need."

Wilbur nibbled a tiny bit of hairy cattypillar.

"Mee-yuck!" He spat it out.

"You'll like it when it's sweetened with sugar," said Winnie.

Wilbur sighed and thought longingly
of tinned tripe with beetles, which was his
favourite food. Wilbur sat down dreamily …
straight onto a patch of stinging nettles.

"You should pick those nettles, not sit
on them!" said Winnie. "They make a
lovely soup."

"Meeeeooooww! Hissss!"

"Oooh, look, a toad!" said Winnie,
parting the long grass. "There he goes!"
Winnie dived like a goalkeeper … and
caught the toad mid-hop.

"Got him!" shouted Winnie. "We'll have
toad-in-the-hole for lunch!"

"**Ribbit!**" went the toad, and it hopped
onto Winnie's head and jumped away.

32

"Quick, chase him!" shouted Winnie, but Wilbur just sat there.

"Oh, all right," said Winnie. "We'll just have hole for lunch, with nettle sauce. Then we'll make that jam."

So Winnie and Wilbur spent all afternoon in the steamy kitchen, stirring cauldrons full of sticky cattypillar jam.

"Tip in more sugar, Wilbur!" said Winnie. She dipped in her wand and gave it a lick. "Eeeek! Ouch! Hot!"

She waved the wand to cool the jam, then licked again.

"Delicious! Have a taste, Wilbur."

Then suddenly Winnie went green. She clutched her tummy.

"Um," she said. "I think I've had enough cattypillars for the moment." She did a big belchy burp.

Chapter Two

Winnie wandered out to see the beautiful red sun and pinky sky behind the upside-down broomstick trees. She soon forgot all about her tummy.

"It's absolutely bee-yoo-ti-ful!" sighed Winnie. She put her hand up to her ear. "Oooh, what was that I heard?"

"**Twooo twit!**"

"That sounded like an owl, but different somehow," said Winnie.

"**Twooo twit!**"

"It must be a rare new kind of owl!" said Winnie. "Oooh, I must take a look at it! Then I can tell Wilbur all about what he's missed!"

Winnie went tiptoeing into the wood.

"**Twooo twit! Twooo twit!**" she called.

Winnie listened. There was silence. She tried again.

"**Twooo twit! Twooo twit! Twooo twit!**"

And this time ...

"**Twooo twit!**" Winnie heard a reply.

"Wow," went Winnie. She could hardly believe it!

"Twooo twit!"

Winnie looked everywhere for the owl.

"Twooo twit!" she called.

"Twooo twit!"

"Where are you, owl?" whispered Winnie.

"Twooo twit!"

"Twooo twit!"

Then, **BUMP!** Winnie walked straight into something big and soft. She bounced off it and went flying.

"Knotted nanny goats!" said Winnie. "What kind of owl can it be?"

"Are you all right, Winnie?" asked a voice from above. It was Jerry, the giant who lived next door.

"Jerry?" said Winnie. "What are you doing out here? Shhh! There's a rare kind of owl nearby, and I've almost caught it!"

"Do you mean an owl that calls backwards?" asked Jerry. He held out a little finger to Winnie and she pulled herself back onto her feet.

"Yes! Have you heard the owl?" whispered Winnie. "I've been calling it, and it's been answering me back!"

"Me too!" said Jerry.

"Ssshh! What do you mean, you too?" asked Winnie.

"I've been calling 'twooo twit' and the owl had been calling back to me," said Jerry.

"Twooo twit? Oh! So, you were the owl!" said Winnie. "That was me calling back, you silly great noodle!"

"Well, you're a twit, too, if you thought I was a bird!" laughed Jerry.

Winnie couldn't help laughing, too. "We could try being birds, if you like," she said. "Would you like to fly, Jerry?"

Before Jerry could say a word, Winnie waved her wand. "**Abracadabra!**"

Chapter Three

Suddenly, both Winnie and Jerry felt something hanging from their shoulders. They had wings!

Jerry flapped his wings, and his big boots lifted off the ground. "I'm flying, Winnie!" he shouted. "I'm flittering and fluttering like a butterfly!"

Jerry's wings were beautiful, but he was a lot bigger and heavier than most butterflies.

Soon, Winnie was up in the sky, too.
Her wings were tatty, black bat wings, like
old umbrellas.

"Wheeee!" yelled Winnie. "I can loop the
loop! I can fly upside down!"

Down below, Wilbur was watching. He
covered his eyes as Winnie looped the loop.
But Winnie was enjoying herself.

"Look at me!" she shouted. "I'm going to
land in a tree!"

But Jerry got to the tree first. **Crump!** He landed on a branch. For a second, everything was quiet, but then creeeeeak … **CRASH!** The branch – and Jerry the butterfly – landed on the ground.

"Ouch!" said Jerry.

A very cross, very ordinary owl flew up from the tree.

"**Twit twooo!**" called the owl.

"Twit yourself!" said Winnie, landing next to Jerry. "Ah, all that fresh air has made me hungry. Do you know what I want to eat?"

Wilbur looked worried.

"What?" said Jerry.

"Absolutely anything as long as it doesn't taste of cattypillar!" said Winnie. "Would you like some jars of cattypillar jam, Jerry?"

"Er …" said Jerry.

"I've got pots of the stuff going free if you'd like it," said Winnie. "I think Wilbur and I are going to open a nice tin of tripe for our tea."

"Purrrr!" said Wilbur, and he licked his lips happily.

After reading activities

Quick quiz

See how fast you can answer these questions! Look back at the stories if you can't remember.

1. In "Blooming Winnie", what does Winnie have to do to grow a new wand?

2. In "Blooming Winnie", what happens when the children see the wand tree?

3. In "Winnie the Twit", who or what is really making the "twooo twit" noise that Winnie hears?

1. plant and water her old wand. 2. they pick the wands and start doing magic. 3. Jerry the giant.

Try This!

★ Design your own magical garden! What amazing plants and creatures will you put in? Draw a picture of your garden and label it with the names of all the magical things.